LIVING HISTORY

THE TUDORS

Tim Pashley

Illustrated by Gerry Wood

Wayland

Living History

The Aztecs
Great Explorers
The Romans

The Saxons
The Tudors
The Vikings

First published in 1985 by
Wayland (Publishers) Ltd
49 Lansdowne Place, Hove,
East Sussex BN3 1HF, England

© Copyright 1985
Wayland (Publishers) Ltd

British Library Cataloguing in
Publication Data

Pashley, Tim
  The Tudors. – (Living history)
  1. England – Social life and customs –
  16th
  century
  I. Title   II. Series
  942.05   DA320

  ISBN 0–85078–698–3

Phototypeset by
Kalligraphics Ltd, Redhill, Surrey
Printed in Italy by
G. Canale & C.S.p.A., Turin
Bound in the U.K. by
The Bath Press, Avon

Picture Acknowledgements:
BBC Hulton, 14; Fotomas Index, 9;
Richard Hook, 19, 20; Open Air
Museum, Singleton, 8; Wayland
Picture Library, 10; all other pictures
by Gerry Wood.

Some of the illustrations
in this book were originally used
in *Elizabeth I and Tudor England*,
in Wayland's Life and Times series.

All the words in the text which
appear in **bold** are explained in the
glossary on page 24.

Contents

Who were the Tudors?

Tudor was the surname of a royal family which ruled over England for 118 years. The first Tudor king was Henry VII. He reigned from 1485 to 1509. Then his son, Henry VIII became king. Henry VIII had six wives. You can see Henry VII and Henry VIII below.

Henry VII
(1485–1509)

Henry VIII
(1509–1547)

Henry VIII's three children, Edward, Mary and Elizabeth, are shown below. Edward was only king for 6 years. He died when he was just 16 years old. Then Mary became queen. She was queen for 5 years. Elizabeth was the last Tudor **monarch**. She ruled from 1558 to 1603. At that time, no woman had ever ruled the country for so long.

Edward VI
(1547–1553)

Mary
(1553–1558)

Elizabeth I
(1558–1603)

Tudor London

In Tudor times London's **population**
was about 200,000.
Today there are 50 times as many
people living in England's capital city.
In the picture you can see Tudor
London's most important buildings.
On the left is the old

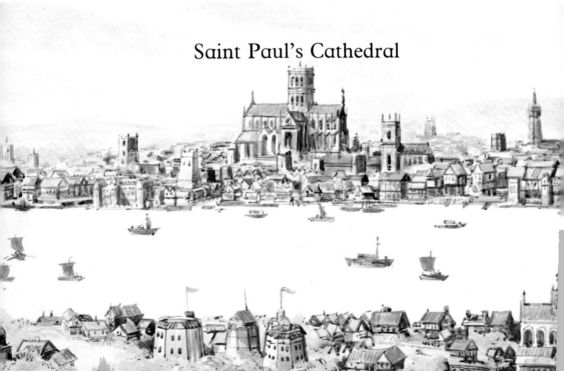

Saint Paul's Cathedral

Saint Paul's Cathedral.
It was the biggest church in London.
You can also see the old London Bridge.
It was the only bridge in the city.
Many houses and shops were
built on the bridge.
On the far right is the Tower of London.
It was so large it was used as a
royal palace, a castle and a prison.

London Bridge

Tower of London

In the country

Most people in Tudor England lived in
small villages or in the countryside.
A Tudor farmer would live in a
house like the one below.
But the farm workers lived in
tiny **wattle and daub** cottages.
They were usually very poor.

Planting crops, harvesting and
keeping animals was the way of life
for nearly everyone.
The weather was very important
to people's lives.
A bad summer meant a poor **harvest**.
People often went hungry in the winter.
The people in the picture are
gathering in the grain harvest.

The Armada

In Tudor times all the countries of
Europe were ruled by royal families.
Sometimes they argued and went to war.
When Elizabeth was queen of England,
the king of Spain sent a fleet of ships,
called the Armada, to **invade** England.
But the English navy **defeated** the
Armada before it reached English shores.
An English warship is shown below.

Here is a scene from the battle.
Sir Francis Drake was one of the
leaders of the English fleet.
Many of the Spanish ships
which escaped were shipwrecked
as they tried to sail home.

Ships and sailing

In Tudor times sailors began to **explore** more of the world.
Sir Francis Drake was the first Englishman to sail around the world.
His ship was called the *Golden Hind*.
Tudor sailing ships were small and took many weeks to sail to Asia or America.
Here is Drake's ship in rough seas.

Above you can see ships being loaded up
at London's **docks** before they sail.
English ships took wool and cloth abroad.
They brought back wine from Europe,
sugar and spices from Asia and
fish and tobacco from America.

Going to church

Almost everyone went to church in Tudor times and you could get into trouble for not going.

The **priest** was one of the most important people in the village.

On the right of the picture below you can see a man being **baptized**. The people on the left are listening to a **sermon**.

Most church services were in **Latin**.

There was much **disagreement** between
Catholics and Protestants and
many people died because of
what they believed about God.
Some people were burnt at the stake,
as the picture above shows.

Health and medicine

Most Tudor people died before they were 45 years old.
People rarely washed.
Streets and houses were very dirty and there were many rats.
Rubbish was thrown out of windows into the streets below.
All this helped disease and illness to spread very quickly.
There were not as many doctors as there are today.

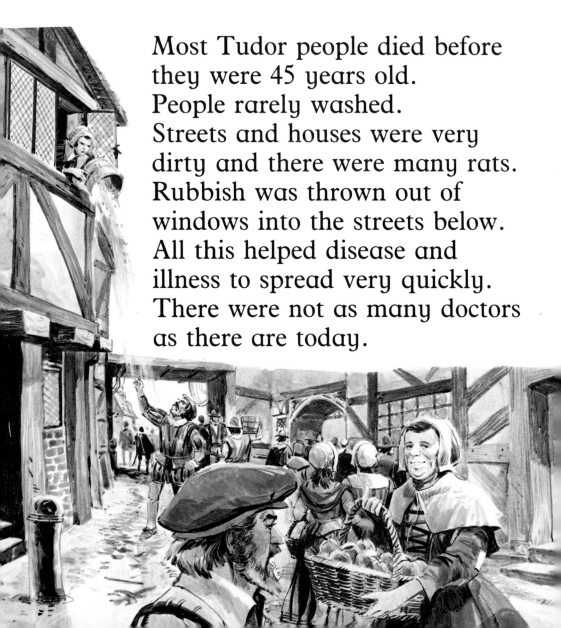

Nobody knew how to cure many of the
illnesses we take medicine for today.
There were no injections to put people
to sleep when they had operations.
They either fainted or had to stay
awake through all the pain.
Doctors often got **barbers** to do
their operations for them.
The man in the picture above
is having his leg **amputated**.

How they dressed

Rich and poor people dressed very
differently in Tudor days.
Wealthy people followed the **fashions** of
the royal family and their **courtiers**.
Ladies' dresses had tight waists and
large padded sleeves and shoulders.
Wide collars called **ruffs** were popular.
Men wore long stockings called hose
and their jackets were called **doublets**.
Trousers were short **breeches**.
All the clothes were brightly coloured.

Ordinary people wore simple clothes
and colours were not so bright.
Coats were large and thick and
tough boots were worn instead of shoes.
Above you can see a man buying
gloves at a market.

At the theatre

Tudor people enjoyed watching plays.
This is the Globe Theatre, beside the
River Thames in Tudor London.
It was England's most famous **theatre**.
It often put on plays by
William Shakespeare.
We still enjoy his plays today.

Here is a scene from a play.
Many plays were stories from the Bible.
There were also history plays and
funny plays called comedies.
If the audience did not like the play or
its actors, they threw rotten vegetables!

Things to do

1. Dressing up

You have read about the clothes that
Tudor people wore.
You have also seen many pictures
of Tudor people.
See if you can find anything among your
own clothes which you could use to dress
up like the Tudors.
Ask someone to take a photograph of you
so that you can see how much you look
like the people in this book.

2. A Tudor farmhouse

Look at the picture on page 12.
Make a model of a Tudor farmhouse out
of a cardboard box.
Put a roof, a chimney, a door and
windows on it.
Now paint your farmhouse.
Make other buildings for your farm.
Find some toy animals to keep on
your Tudor farm.

Glossary

Amputate   To cut off an arm or leg if it is badly injured.

Baptism   A religious ceremony performed in Christian churches.

Barber   A person who cuts hair and shaves beards.

Breeches   Short trousers fastened below the knees.

Courtier   A member of a king or queen's court.

Defeat   To beat somebody in a battle or a fight.

Disagree   To have different thoughts about something or to quarrel with somebody.

Dock   A place where ships are loaded, unloaded or mended.

Doublet   A short men's jacket.

Explore   To look carefully round a place.

Fashion   Up-to-date clothes worn by people to look smart.

Harvest   Gathering in the crops at the end of summer.

Invade   To try to capture a country by sending soldiers to take it over.

Latin   The language spoken by the ancient Romans.

Monarch   A king, queen, emperor or empress.

Population   The number of people living in a place.

Priest   A person who is in charge of a church.

Ruff   A large collar round the top of a shirt or blouse.

Sermon   A talk given in church.

Theatre   A place where people watch plays or shows.

Wattle and daub   Interwoven twigs and clay, used for building in Tudor times.

Books to read

Living in the Elizabethan Court by R.J. Unstead (A & C Black, 1975)
Queen Elizabeth I by Betka Zamoyska (Longman, 1981)
Sir Francis Drake by Edyth Harper (Ladybird, 1977)
The Tudor Family by Ann Mitchell (Wayland, 1972)
Tudor People by John Fines (Batsford, 1977)
William Shakespeare by Dorothy Turner (Wayland, 1985)

Index